T0065687

GOD'S
CHOSEN
REBEL

KATHY SHERIDAN

WESTBOW
PRESS®
A DIVISION OF THOMAS NELSON
& ZONDERVAN

WestBow Press books may be ordered through booksellers or by contacting:

WestBow Press
A Division of Thomas Nelson & Zondervan
1663 Liberty Drive
Bloomington, IN 47403
www.westbowpress.com
844-714-3454

Because of the dynamic nature of the Internet, any web addresses or
links contained in this book may have changed since publication and
may no longer be valid. The views expressed in this work are solely those
of the author and do not necessarily reflect the views of the publisher,
and the publisher hereby disclaims any responsibility for them.

Any people depicted in stock imagery provided by Getty Images are models,
and such images are being used for illustrative purposes only.
Certain stock imagery © Getty Images.

Scripture quotations are from the Holy Bible, King James Version
(Authorized Version). First published in 1611. Quoted from the KJV Classic
Reference Bible, Copyright © 1983 by The Zondervan Corporation.

ISBN: 978-1-6642-9128-7 (sc)
ISBN: 978-1-6642-9129-4 (e)

Library of Congress Control Number: 2023901863

Print information available on the last page.

WestBow Press rev. date: 04/10/2023

INTRODUCTION

Most of us learn from our own mistakes and occasionally from the mistakes of others. God uses stories in the Bible for us to learn from. In one of the unusual stories, Jonah's defiant behavior caused him to tour around the sea on an unexpected and unpleasant journey. God's purposes were fulfilled in spite of Jonah's willful disobedience.

Some of us like to pick and choose those we think are worthy of God's love and those who aren't. Like Jonah, we find ourselves rebellious and stubborn, living in our own selfish world. God wishes that no one will perish, and he calls us to go and share His love with others and show them the way to salvation. Because of Jonah's defiant behavior, God put him through severe and harsh discipline. The punishment almost cost him his life. After everything Jonah went through, he still did not want to share God's love with a sinful group of people. If we can learn to live God's way, we will save ourselves from going down a path of pain and suffering.

God is looking for someone willing to set aside their personal wants and desires and tell others about the love of Him and the forgiveness of sins. There is a broad path that leads to destruction and a narrow one that leads to salvation. Make it your purpose to tell others about His love.

All scripture used in this book comes from the King James Bible. Due to copyrights, entire books in the Bible are not permitted to be copied. From chapters 1 through 4 in this book, the scriptures are paraphrased.

Prayers are written in the singular form, making them personal. Otherwise, the plural form is used.

When speaking of God in various forms, the words will be capitalized, but when speaking of Jonah, they will not be capitalized unless used at the beginning of a sentence.

PRAYER

Heavenly Father,

I come boldly to your throne of grace and mercy with praise and thanksgiving in my heart. I am seeking to find out who you are and what is required of me. Your word is written to gain wisdom, knowledge, and instruction for daily living. By obeying your word, I can live an abundant life. Life is miserable if I choose to live in rebellion against you. Help me choose to live a life that will bring honor and glory to you. The way I live here on earth counts all the way to eternity.

Help me choose to give my life to serving you, as I lean on your strength to lay down my selfish desires. It's only by living for you that I can be truly satisfied. Help me to bring honor and glory to your name, as I choose to serve you and not myself. Help me take a journey through your word and learn from the examples others have made. Thank you in Jesus' name. Amen

CHAPTER 1

When God came to Jonah, He wanted him to go and speak to the people of Nineveh and warn them about their wicked behavior. Rather than do what God asked, Jonah hopped on board a ship and headed to Tarshish, trying to flee from the presence of God. Jonah 1:1-3 (paraphrased KJV)

In the first three verses of Jonah, chapter 1, we see that God called Jonah for a specific reason, and he heard His voice loud and clear. Rather than obey, he came up with his own plan. By running, he thought God would leave him alone. Jonah was called to warn the people of Nineveh about their great sin. He didn't realize the dangerous detour that was ahead or the total cost of his disobedience.

We too, like stubborn Jonah, can disrespect the call that God places on our lives. We think that by running, God will somehow forget about what He told us to do. What price are you willing to pay to get away from God? It almost cost Jonah his life. God wants us to learn to hear His voice and obey Him. His call on all of us is to go and preach the gospel and bring others to know Him. There are people we encounter who may only know about Jesus because we took the time to tell them of His love.

The people of Nineveh were in desperate need of a savior. Their wicked sin was so great, yet they had no clue that destruction was knocking at their door. They didn't realize how desperate they were for someone to show them the love and mercy of God. God called that rebellious Jonah to be the salt and light so the people of Nineveh would repent of their sins and come to know Him. In spite of Jonah's resistance and stubbornness, God was able to work through the turn of events and use them for His glory.

PRAYER

Heavenly Father,

I am coming to your throne with praise and thanksgiving in my heart. I am grateful and blessed for all that you have done for me. You don't speak to me with a loud voice, but you speak to my heart in a still, small voice. Help me listen to your voice that whispers my name with clear directions. Fine-tune my hearing so that I can hear you as I ignore all other voices bidding for my attention. Give me the strength to obey when I hear you tell me what to do. Please help me not to run away from the call you have placed on my life. It is only by living for you that I will be truly happy. Help me not to be tempted to go in the wrong direction. Teach me how to reach the lost with your love. Thank you, Father, in Jesus' name. Amen

God sent out a great windstorm, causing a powerful disturbance, so the ship Jonah was on was about to be destroyed. Fellow shipmates were afraid, so they cried out to their gods to save them while throwing stuff on the ship overboard, trying to lighten the load. Undisturbed by the commotion, Jonah was found sleeping. He was rudely awakened by the ship master, who told him to arise and call upon his God so that his God might keep them from perishing. Jonah 1:4-6 (paraphrased)

Sometimes, in order for God to get our attention, He will allow complete chaos to come into our lives. Others may see the disasters we are walking into while we remain ignorant. Jonah slept on, unaware of the fear the crewmen felt, knowing the storm was about to destroy the ship and everyone on board. Being ignorant of the real power of God, the men frantically called out to their powerless gods to save them as they started throwing things off the ship. No false god or anything else they tried stopped the raging sea.

Nothing is too difficult for God; He is able to hear and change our circumstances through His great power. Finding Jonah asleep, the captain demanded to know how he could be sleeping while turmoil was raging all around. Jonah was also ordered to call out to his God so that He might save them. Jonah could not run from or sleep his way out of the call that God put on his life. Waking up, he realized God wasn't fooled; he had only deceived himself.

PRAYER

Heavenly Father,

I come to your throne of grace and mercy with praise and thanksgiving on my lips and in my heart. Please help me to take this walk with you seriously, correct me when I am wrong, and help me not ignore your voice when you tell me what to do. I want to be corrected by you, and I want to be obedient to your will. Don't let me get away with anything that is not pleasing to you. Help me to always be sensitive, knowing that you can become disappointed in my behavior, grieving you and the Holy Spirit. You have given me a choice: to live for you or for myself. Living for you means getting my mind off of myself and doing something for others. I am aware that all my gifts and talents were given to me by you and that they are to be used for your glory, not mine. Loving you is obeying you. Thank you in Jesus' name. Amen

The men on board decided to cast lots in order to find out who was responsible for the raging storm that was upon them. The lot fell on Jonah. Everyone on board demanded Jonah tell them why this trouble was upon them. They also wanted to know what he did for a living, where he came from, and why he brought this evil upon them. Jonah admitted that he was a Hebrew and feared God and that God was the creator of heaven and earth. Because Jonah admitted he was fleeing from God, the men became fearful. Jonah 1:7-10 (paraphrased)

Others knew Jonah was fleeing from God because he told them. We can become a stumbling block to unbelievers when they see us as hypocrites. We see Jonah confessing he knew God when confronted; otherwise, he would have stayed asleep until the ship landed.

Unconvinced that there was a raging storm for no reason, lots were cast to find out who was responsible for the turmoil that was upon them. No doubt the lot hit the right target; Jonah was the man. Pointing fingers at Jonah's misconduct, everyone on board wanted to know who he was, where he came from, and the reason for his irresponsible actions.

Jonah had to give an account to God and others for his callous behavior. It was a wake-up call for everyone, and Jonah had no choice but to face the consequences of his carelessness. The men on board cried out to their gods, who could do nothing for them, and here was a man telling them that he feared God but was running from Him. Causing panic among everyone, the men now knew why the storm was upon them and also that God was dealing with Jonah. Fearing for their lives, the men questioned Jonah, "Why hast thou done this?" Jonah 1:10

God knows our location at all times. We can't run and hide from Him; there is no place where He is not. If we're not willing to obey God when He tells us what to do, He can and will oftentimes use others to confront us. If we're heading in the wrong direction, He will do whatever it takes to get our attention. God will never waver in His love for us, but disobedience and running from Him cause unnecessary pain, heartache, and misery. We carry a heavy weight of guilt around when we choose disobedience.

PRAYER

Dear God,

Thank you that I can come to your throne today with praise and thanksgiving as I seek your presence and guidance. Let me not take you for granted, thinking I have the right to stomp on your goodness. It's only by your grace and mercy that I can receive your forgiveness for the times I choose to live for myself. There is no place I can hide from you; even my thoughts speak loud and clear to you. It's only in believing and obeying that my life can be lived to its fullest potential. True happiness can only come while living by your word and doing what it tells me to do. Remind me that you go wherever I go, and you see the reasons for everything I do. I cannot outsmart you, and I don't ever want to think my ways are better than yours. Please help me to keep my eyes on you and be obedient to your voice. Help keep me from unnecessary detours and distractions that beg for my attention trying to pull me away from you.

Thank you in Jesus' name. Amen

With a furious storm raging, Jonah was asked what was to be done so that the sea would become calm. Jonah once again told them that it was his fault that the storm was upon them and that by tossing him into the sea, the storm would calm. Not wanting to harm Jonah, the men continued to row harder, trying to bring the ship to land. Every effort done within their own power was no match. The sea fought against them, making all their efforts useless. Jonah 1:11-13 (paraphrased)

The decisions we make affect not only us but others as well. Jonah's disobedience put others' lives in danger. By his own admission, everyone on board was aware that this Hebrew man was the cause of the evil that was upon them. Jonah told them if they threw him overboard, the sea would stop raging. With gripping fear, desperation, panic, and exhaustion, nothing done in their own strength matched the raging storm. Try as they might, they were unable to maneuver the ship and bring it to safety. The fearful men tried harder to save their lives and Jonah's, but the sea's turmoil wouldn't allow them to make land. They eventually realized that no matter how hard they tried, their strength and efforts were useless.

Most of the time, we find out the hard way that we are not as smart as we think, and without God, we can't do anything. Our own self-serving plans and trying to outsmart God are not wise; they only cause bigger messes. By blaming others or God, we deceive ourselves into believing we're not responsible for our actions.

When we cry out to God and He tells us what to do, like it or not, He doesn't change His mind. God doesn't think the way we do. His ways are beyond ours, and they don't have to always make sense to us. He is omnipresent and sees the whole picture; we only see life from our own perspective. If we think we are something we're not, we only deceive ourselves.

PRAYER

Father in Heaven,

Thank you for loving me. Help me lean on your wisdom and strength, knowing I am weak without you. My ways are not your ways, and I can do nothing without you. Help me to stay on your straight and narrow path that leads to life. I don't want to deceive myself into believing that I am better than someone else. I don't want to do things my way if it leads down a path of destruction. Do what you have to do to change the direction of my life if I choose to go astray. Thank you in Jesus' name. Amen

The men called out to God, pleading for His mercy. They begged Him not to let them perish for the sake of Jonah or be accountable for his demise. Trying to please the Lord, they took Jonah and tossed him overboard. As soon as he fell into the water, the sea calmed down and the raging ceased. Being fearful of God, the men made vows and offered sacrifices to Him. Jonah 1:14-16 (paraphrased)

Doing what God tells us to do is what works out for our best. These unbelievers saw that God was dealing with Jonah's rebellion. Unaware God was planning to save Jonah, they knew throwing him overboard would surely end his life. Not wanting to be responsible for Jonah's demise, they begged and pleaded with God not to let them perish or hold them accountable for Jonah's death. By doing what Jonah told them they should do, throwing him overboard, they witnessed the power of God when the sea stopped raging. In awe of God's ability to calm the waters and save them, they made sacrifices to Him.

God uses everything we do to work out for His glory, and He wants no one to perish. Jonah had no idea that God used his defiant rebellion to shake these people and be a witness to them. Not because of anything Jonah did, but because of what they saw God do. God used the circumstance they found themselves in as an opportunity for them to come to know Him, the creator of heaven and earth. They too were on a path of destruction because of their belief in false gods. For the first time, they saw the power of the one true God, and for the first time in their lives, they feared Him. This may have been their only opportunity to encounter the powerful God in heaven.

PRAYER

Dear Heavenly Father,

Thank you that I can be a vessel used to win souls for your kingdom. I need to be willing to share the good news of your love and salvation message with others. Remind me not to get impatient with the process as you draw out the unsaved in your infinite timing. Thank you for your patience during my stubborn years when I wanted nothing to do with you. Help me remember that everyone deserves to know that your love covers their sin. Help me be sensitive when sharing your love. Show me when to speak and when to back off and be quiet. Everyone's journey is different; there are some who just need more time than others. When I do open my mouth, help me speak words that come from you and are seasoned from above. I do not want to force-feed your word on anyone. I do not want to think that I am better than anyone else, so please help me not to use harsh words that may cause someone to turn away from your invitation for salvation. Remind me that I am accountable for my actions, and I can take no credit for your glory. I need wisdom from the throne of heaven to carry your presence wherever I go. Help me not to become a stumbling block to anyone. Thank you in Jesus' name. Amen

God prepared an enormous fish to swallow Jonah. For three days and nights, Jonah was kept alive and sheltered in the belly of the fish. Jonah 1:17 (paraphrased)

God doesn't always provide for our needs the way we think He should. His timing is perfect, and He uses everything for His glory. In His grace and mercy, God spared Jonah's life by providing a fish to swallow him. He wasn't given a five-star luxury hotel suite with penthouse accommodations, but rather an out-of-the-ordinary means of survival. Jonah must have felt uncomfortable, perplexed, and terrified when the big fish swallowed him. The nauseating smell and the darkness had to be haunting.

Although God's protection seemed momentary, Jonah had no idea how long he would be in the situation he found himself in. One way or the other, defeat seemed to be calling his name: death by digestion, or the fish could spit him out to fight the sea's elements.

None of us can come close to knowing what it was like to slosh around in the belly of a slimy fish, barred from the outside world. As gross and disgusting as Jonah's situation was, he didn't see the need for an attitude adjustment, and he wasn't happy about his perplexing circumstances. Jonah felt helpless, hopeless and trapped. God used this horrifying situation to get his attention, giving him time to think about what he was running from. This must have felt like cruel punishment and an unusual trick from God. But it was an opportunity for Jonah to have a change of heart.

PRAYER

Dear Jesus,

Thank you for your loving kindness that examines my heart and helps me change into someone who glorifies you. Please help me keep in mind that you see everything, and help me not to think that I can run and hide anything from you. Help me remember that your word says that my sin will find me out, so don't let me get away with anything. Interrupt my plans if I am going in the wrong direction. Thank you for loving me. Amen

CHAPTER 2

Crying out from a unique position of punishment, Jonah prayed to God while in the belly of the fish. Feeling like he was in the pit of hell, he knew God had heard his prayer. Pouting about his troubles, Jonah blamed God for throwing him into the deep sea. He felt like the waves were closing in. Out of desperation, he felt like the flooding water and the weeds were choking him, so Jonah decided to talk to God. On his own, there was no escaping from the despair he was in. Jonah 2:1-6 (paraphrased)

Thank God, there's no place to go and hide where He can't find us. Jonah was over his head in hopelessness, not knowing if God was going to save him from this horrifying place of dread. Praying and expecting a miracle was his only hope. In complete desperation and feeling like he was in the pit of hell, Jonah prayed in tormenting darkness, facing unknown fear.

At Jonah's lowest point of despair, he knew he had to have a supernatural, divine miracle because no one but God knew where he was. There was also no one but God who could save him from the mess he was in. Choose defeat or pray to God for help. In utter agony, he sought God, and his prayers were answered from the surrounding depths of darkness.

God wants to have daily fellowship with us, not just when things are bad. When we pray, we have to trust that God hears us and then believe He is working on our behalf. Jonah's life was over if God didn't intercede. Out of ignorance and our own stubbornness, sometimes we have to come to the end of ourselves before we are willing to ask God for help. He promises to never leave us or forsake us. All we have to do is cry out to Him, and He hears us. He kept Jonah in the pit of tormenting darkness and terror until he came to his senses. When we are in emotional situations, real or imaginary, we have to put our trust in God. If we love Him and seek Him, He will work all things out for our good.

PRAYER

Dear God,

Thank you for making it so I don't have to be falling apart to talk to you. Thank you for using Jonah's story to show me that running from you causes unnecessary heartache and misery. I trust that you know what's best for me, and you will love me through whatever I am facing. I don't want to

take my eyes off of you and go astray.
Daily, I want to seek your will for my
life because you know me better than I
know myself, and I am nothing without
you. My ways lead me to unwanted
disasters; your ways lead to a life with
more abundance. Help me to lean on
you and be thankful for everything. In
Jesus' name. Amen

When Jonah came to his senses and remembered to pray, he reached into God's holy presence. Don't believe your own deceitful lies and forsake the mercy of God. Always pray, give a sacrifice of thanksgiving, and pay your vows. Salvation comes from God. In His mercy, God told the fish to throw Jonah out onto dry land. Jonah 2:7-10 (paraphrased)

As Jonah sloshed around in the belly of the fish, he decided to pray with thankfulness. What a prayer closet! with no one else around, just him talking to God. He reached rock bottom and was powerless to help himself if God didn't show up. He faced gloom, doom, and death if the fish digested him or spit him out into the danger of the sea. Surrounded by desperation with no available rescue, God was the only one who could speak to his pathetic agony and change the dire situation. God, in His infinite wisdom, mercy, and grace, intervened and spoke to the fish.

God uses every situation in our lives, orchestrating, arranging, or directing every detail of our circumstances to get our attention. He changed the weather, provided the fish at the right time, and kept Jonah in the pit until he asked Him for help. Thankfully, the fish wasn't a rebel like Jonah. When God spoke, the fish obeyed. Being kept from the dangers of the sea, God supernaturally guided the fish to dry land, where he regurgitated Jonah.

PRAYER

Father,

Thank you for helping me keep a humble heart in all the circumstances I find myself in. You will never put me through more than I can handle, but I can put myself in situations where, without your help, I will drown in my own miserable messes. I want to live my life so that it pleases you. Doing things my way makes life more difficult than it has to be. Help me to recognize what grieves you and the Holy Spirit. I don't want to be stubborn and live only to please myself. There are others who need to know that your love is for them also. Today, I am determined to choose your ways over mine. Thank you in Jesus' name. Amen

CHAPTER 3

God's word came a second time and spoke to Jonah. He was to rise up and go to Nineveh and preach to the people only what the Lord wanted him to say. This time, when God said to go, Jonah took the three three-day journey to the great city of Nineveh. Jonah 3:1-3 (paraphrased)

God knew what needed to be done before calling Jonah for the job. His purpose was fulfilled, even though Jonah fought hard not to do what God asked him to do. Nineveh desperately needed someone to show them that their lifestyle wasn't pleasing to God. Jonah was chosen for the job, regardless of his anger and resentment. He was still used by God to proclaim liberty to a sinful city.

God didn't waver or change His mind; His call was still there. Determined to get Jonah to obey, God told him the same thing He had already told him before: "Arise, go unto Nineveh, that great city, and preach unto it the preaching that I bid thee." Jonah 3:2 Throwing temper tantrums and pouting did not persuade God to see things the way Jonah saw them. He didn't excuse Jonah's bad behavior, nor did He feel sorry for him. God's ways and thoughts are higher than ours, and Jonah learned the hard way that God gave him no wiggle room. He wasn't let off the hook just because he didn't want to go or because God thought he had suffered too much already. Jonah had a rude awakening when God expected him to obey His call.

Jonah already spent three days on an unwanted, no-sightseeing cruise, touring and flopping around in the belly of a fish. He was faced with another agonizing three-day walk to Nineveh. If nothing else, he learned the hard way that trying to escape did him no good.

PRAYER

Dear Jesus,

Thank you and praise you. When you place a call on my life, remind me that you are there to help me through whatever it is you want me to do. I will not be left without your guidance. I want to listen and hear you so I can say what you want me to say and go where you want me to go. I can do all things through you by leaning on your strength. Thank you. Amen

As Jonah entered the city, he told the people that in forty days, Nineveh would be destroyed. All the people of Nineveh proclaimed a fast, put on sackcloth, and believed in God.
Jonah 3:4-5 (paraphrased)

God works in mysterious ways, and He is the only one who knows if the salvation message before Jonah's ordeal would have impacted the people as it did after. Nineveh was in desperate need of someone to show them their lifestyle was not pleasing to God. Entering the city, the poor, wretched Jonah spoke a simple but stern message from God, and the people believed. By warning the people, Jonah changed the course of a city headed for eternal damnation into one seeking God through prayer and fasting.

Jonah's raggedy appearance had to be a horrifying sight, incredibly grotesque and hideous. His repugnant hygiene had to be utterly repulsive, and everything about his appearance spoke as loudly as his verbal message. Somehow the people knew that Jonah wrestled with God and God won. Apparently, they didn't want to end up like this man. If God sent this hideous-looking person to warn them about the destruction to come, it was time to repent.

PRAYER

Heavenly Father,

    If I am to be a servant to you, I have to be willing to obey your call on my life. Never let me take you for granted, believing that you will just look the other way if I don't want to do what you tell me to do. I want to be a light that shines in the darkness so that others will seek you. Help me speak words that are seasoned from above and spoken in your timing. Help me not to be judgmental or get in the way of someone's walk with you. Words spoken at the right moment will bring joy; words spoken at the wrong time without compassion will cause more damage than good. Help me to use kind words when I tell someone of your love. Thank you in Jesus' name. Amen

When the king of Nineveh got the word, he took off his priestly robe, put on uncomfortable sackcloth, and sat in ashes. He sent out an order announcing that no person or animal of any kind was allowed to eat or drink water. Everyone had to be covered in sackcloth, cry out to God, and turn from their evil and violent ways. The people were hoping that God would hear them and turn from His anger against them so that they wouldn't perish. When God saw that they were serious and that they stopped their evil ways, He changed His mind and decided not to destroy them. Jonah 3:6-10 (paraphrased)

Jonah didn't have to do anything spectacular; he just showed up and told the people to repent and turn from their wicked ways. The entire community took Jonah's message to heart. By the order of the king's decree, they did everything they could to seek God and change their ways. Because the people repented and turned away from their evilness, God turned away from the destruction that He planned against them and spared their lives. The man Jonah changed the course of a sinful city into believing in God because he finally obeyed and did what God asked him to do. God wants no one to perish. His timing was perfect for the sinful people of Nineveh. They were ready to receive the message that God had for them. Thank God He was still able to use Jonah's delayed obedience for His glory.

PRAYER

Father,

I, too, like Jonah, can become stubborn and unwilling to do what you want me to do if it doesn't fit into my plans. I need your help to change my attitude when I have little to no compassion for someone. I want to see others through your eyes, and I am asking for a heart that wants to see the lost saved. Your word says that you wish no one would perish. If I allow bitterness, anger, and hatred to enter my heart toward others, then I'm no good at what I'm called to do. Show me who needs a special touch from you today, and help me show your kindness and love as I speak of you. "Life and death are in the power of my tongue." I need your help to choose my words wisely so that I don't offend someone you are trying to reach. Thank you in Jesus' name. Amen

CHAPTER 4

Jonah was extremely furious, trying to excuse himself for fleeing. He reminds our gracious Lord that he had prayed before, but He didn't listen. He knew that God is slow to anger and wanted to pour out His mercy, grace, and kindness toward the sinners of Nineveh. God was willing to forgive their sins, but Jonah wanted nothing to do with God's plan for these people, begging for God to let him die and not live. God let Jonah know it was OK for him to be angry. Jonah 4:1-4 (paraphrased)

Jonah paid a giant price for his disobedience, and he was still bitter and mad that God wanted to forgive the people and save them from their sins. Jonah never appeared grateful, had a change of heart, or thanked God for saving his life and rescuing him from a dreadful situation. Causing his own self-inflicted pain, the ruthless rebel grudgingly obeyed. Forgetting about the unmerited favor of God's love during his time of desperation, he still didn't think the people deserved God's mercy and grace. Jonah had no compassion for the lost souls of Nineveh, telling God he wanted to die rather than see the Ninevites repent and know Him. He just didn't get it; God's mercy and grace are for everyone, not just for Jonah and the ones he thought were worthy.

PRAYER

Father,

Thank you for saving me. Thank you that I can rejoice when others come to know you. Correct me if I ever become high-minded, thinking I'm better than someone else or that they don't deserve to know about your love and saving grace. Thank you for not giving up on me and helping me stay rooted and grounded in your love. Knock me out with the power of the Holy Spirit, if that's what it takes for me to be obedient, and help me find joy in being a witness for you. I was lost without you, and I never want to forget that. Help me want salvation for the lost. Remind me that it's my job to love people, pray for them, and tell them about the opportunity to come and know you. I want to have a teachable heart and do what you want me to do so that you won't have to ask

someone else to take my place. Please
help me not to get jealous of what you
are doing for others. Please help me to
trust that I can be your hands and feet
to share your word with the lost.
Thank you in Jesus' name. Amen

**Jonah departed to the east side of the city, where he made a
booth to keep himself shaded. He waited around to see what
was going to happen to the city. Jonah was glad when God
made a gourd for his comfort and covering. The next day,
when a worm struck the gourd, it dried up and withered.
Emotional Jonah fainted and wished himself to die. God told
him that it did him well to be angry because he had pity on a
gourd that grew overnight and perished. God reminded him
that there were more than one hundred and twenty thousand
people who needed rescuing and didn't know right from
wrong. Jonah 4:5-11 (paraphrased)**

Jonah's thoughts were twisted, and God wasn't
through dealing with his rebellion. He was a racist
rebel; his actions and words spoke volumes about
the condition of his hard heart. Jonah had a big ME
problem and continued to argue with God because he
didn't want to do what was asked of him. After his
horrific nightmare, Jonah never appeared thankful or
grateful, nor did he have any sympathy for the lost souls
God wanted him to reach.

Jonah's narcissistic, superior, and insulting behavior
caused him to think life revolved around him and what
he wanted. He only saw life through his own eyes and not
through God's. He allowed ugly pride to stand in the way

when he put himself in a position of judgment. Believing himself better than the unworthy sinners of Nineveh, he thought that they deserved nothing but damnation. Jonah was still mad at God for His decision to save these people from destruction; he deemed them undeserving of God's love and mercy. He wanted to die rather than see salvation for these people, hoping God would change His mind and destroy them.

With God orchestrating Jonah's disaster and saving him from demise, somehow his thinking never changed about the call on his life. Jonah was hoping God wouldn't have pity on those undeserving sinners, all the while watching and hoping they would perish. Once again, God, in His mercy and grace, provided Jonah with supernatural shelter. The gourd was made for his comfort, and he became angry and wished to die when it shriveled. He had more pity for a shriveled-up gourd than for the lost souls of Nineveh, not wanting to bother himself about it.

We become stinky when our ugly selfishness rears its head and disregards the needs of others. How soon did Jonah forget the agony of his own horrifying experience? Living in the belly of a large fish should have changed his way of thinking, but he only seemed more resentful toward God. **One good thing about Jonah is that he never lied to God. Doing himself no good, he continued to grumble, complain, and point his finger at God, verbalizing how he felt.**

PRAYER

Father,

I come to your throne to thank you for saving me. You don't want anyone to perish, and my job is to win souls for your kingdom and not chase anyone away. Help me not to grow weary in doing what you want me to do or get discouraged and disappointed when others don't want to accept you. You created us and know the experiences and depths of everyone's soul. I am asking for a compassionate heart as I tell someone about you because I don't know what they might be struggling with. I may be the one to plant a seed in someone's heart or the one to water it. All plants need different amounts of nurturing, but they will die without water or drown with too much. Send me to do the job you want me to do, nothing more and nothing less. Keep me humble and keep me from a religious attitude, coming across as though I am better than someone else. I do not want to be the reason someone doesn't want to know you. I have to remember that it is your work, done in your way and timing. Your love goes beyond my perception. I never want to be so high-minded or judgmental, believing that your love is for me and only those I deem worthy. I am not here to beat the word over anyone's head or to judge them for the decisions they choose to make. Your plans are greater than mine, and I am not in authority over someone's life, nor am I sent by you to force your love down anyone's throat. It is not by my might or my power but by your spirit that you draw others to repentance. All the glory belongs to you and not me. There are people in my life that I am called to show your love to. It's not my job to deem them unworthy. If you are exalted, you will call others unto you. I need to be corrected if my attitude is not pleasing to you. Help me find and fulfill the call that you have placed on my life. Don't let me get distracted by the cares of this world or be afraid to share your love. It's more important what you think of me than what others may think. My job is to love others and want what's best for them. Thank you in Jesus' name. Amen

CONCLUSION

Salvation is for everyone, and it is not in God's will for anyone to perish. God created us in His image and loves everyone with unconditional love, which is why Jesus went to the cross. He died for everyone's sins, and we have no authority to pick and choose who is worthy of His love. We are the salt, and we are called to let our light shine before others so that they will glorify God. Let God's love rest on you, so that others will see and want what you have. Are you living like the world, having no fruit of joy, love, or compassion for anyone but yourself? Living for God means laying down your desires so that others may know Him.

Is there something in your life that is getting in the way of what God is calling you to do? Self-doubt, unwillingness, or something else causes you to change the direction God has for you. God has reasons for choosing you. If God entrusts you with a task, He will equip and train you for the job. If God is happy to send you to do a job, then embrace it and run with it. He knows what you are capable of doing. While trying to outsmart our Creator's wisdom and strength, Jonah was faced with a death-defying battle and still had to obey. Be willing to obey before God has to take drastic measures to get your attention. Our own plans cause more pain and heartache than necessary.

God tailor-made each one of us and has called us to impact others for Him. He is looking for someone willing to set aside their personal desires and go tell others about the forgiveness of sin, even when it's not comfortable or easy. Be that someone who believes God has His plan to save the lost. You may be the only one who can reach another with the love of God, so don't miss an opportunity. It is a tragedy for anyone to enter eternity without the love of God. Running and hiding from God is not an option; He knows more about us than we do about ourselves. He knows our thoughts and how many hairs are on our heads. My business is to do what God wants me to do, whether I like it or not.

The way we talk to God speaks a lot about the condition of our hearts. Do you only talk to Him when you're in need, then forget about Him when times are good? Are your prayers selfish, always about what you want and what it takes to make you happy? Do you forget to pray for or help others with greater needs than yours? God's greatest desire is for us to talk to Him about everything because His love goes beyond our understanding. Don't be a person who always complains about how unfair life is for you. Be thankful and grateful for what God wants to do in your life, especially if you need to be corrected. He cares so much for us that He wants us to behave in a way that glorifies Him.

Stubbornness allows life to throw us into a tailspin, causing unnecessary turmoil and chaos. Does God's guidance resolve problems for you and lead you into a more abundant life? When situations take our lives on an unexpected journey, we can be left with struggling thoughts, blaming, and asking God, "Why?" When we don't understand the situation we're faced with, we can lean on God's peace that passes all understanding. He sees the big picture and is working everything out for the good of those who believe. We need to ask for God's wisdom when life doesn't make sense.

Never think you're smarter than God, believing you know what's best for your life. Make it easy for yourself and know that God comes out the winner in every circumstance. Stop trying to do things your way and hope God will bless you. For some unknown reason, most of us think we can handle our own lives and are too stubborn or proud to call on God. God sees the heart, and He knows every motive for why we do what we do. When telling others about God, pray that the condition of any bad attitude you might have won't cause someone to stumble. Believe that the message of God is what they hear and not be focused on your demeanor.

Do you find it hard to celebrate when God pours out His favor on someone other than yourself? Is judging or criticizing a choice on your menu, based on what you think someone deserves or how they behave? God's grace and mercy go beyond our way of thinking. We need to humble ourselves and ask God to forgive our wicked hearts and teach us to have more compassion for others.

Be thankful that God sees someone's heart and doesn't judge them on their outward appearance. There are ways that seem right to us, but doing things our own way can lead to destruction. We need to seek God's perspective, making sure we have His wisdom before we open our mouths and say something unwise.

We think that by running away somehow God is going to forget about what He told us to do, but He doesn't repent nor change His mind. Unwillingness and complete disrespect for God's call may cause Him to take drastic measures to get our attention. If making our lives uncomfortable doesn't work, God may choose something more miserable until we realize His ways are higher than ours. Learning to obey quickly will save us from a lot of unnecessary heartaches. God tells us to love our enemies and pray for them. We have to remember that it is because of God's mercy that we ourselves are not consumed. Those who seem to be living a good life without God are headed for some unseen disaster, not realizing it is a recipe for misery. Give God permission to do whatever it takes to correct you.

Don't try to figure God out; it doesn't do you any good to be angry at Him for wanting to use you. Let it go; rejoice that He wants to use you for His glory. Be glad that someone might not perish because of you. What happened to Jonah's hard heart can happen to us. Ask God to help you get rid of your anger, bitterness, and resentment toward Him and others. Our enemies are not God's. He tells us to love, pray for, and do good to them. Don't be Jonah, casting your unworthy opinions where they don't belong. Jonah was sleeping on the job; napping was his choice of drug, his way of escaping reality. Wake up, stop procrastinating, and get going with what God wants you to do.

Vengeance belongs to the Lord, and He will repay. It's not our job to try and get even with someone who hurts us, thinking they deserve payback. Don't be malicious, waiting to see if God will punish others for their mistakes because that's what we think they have coming. We can become like Jonah, not wanting God's love for someone because we deem them unfit. Is there someone you don't want God to have mercy on, and you're hoping they perish in their sin because of your misguided opinion of them? Repent and ask God to forgive you for your wrongful way of thinking, and ask Him to give you a new heart of compassion. Let Him show you ways to bless and not curse others.

Don't be high-minded, praising your own greatness, or thinking you are better than someone else. God's love is for everyone, not just the few we feel deserve it. We were all at one time blind and now see through the grace and mercy of God. Be glad that someone took the time to pray for you or told you about the love of your Savior. Maybe they didn't feel like it or didn't think you deserved God's love, but they went ahead and led you to the way, the truth, and the life. Now it's your turn to show others that eternity is forever, and God wants to spend it with them.

How often do we pass judgment, misdiagnose someone's situation, and give up on them because they seem beyond help or hope? We aren't who we say we are if we pass by or turn away those in need of our help because we don't want to get involved with their problems. By pushing away those who are broken and hurting, we may be driving them deeper into despair and hopelessness. Pray that your life is an example of God's love and not a reason for someone to reject His goodness. Jonah saw himself as better than the people who needed God's compassion and didn't want to offer them His redemption. Those we are called to love may only be in our lives for a season. But in that season, God has a plan for you to show them the way. You might be the first one to share the gospel message with someone, or maybe you're reinforcing a message they've already heard. Either way, it's our job to let others know that Jesus loves them. It's not by our might nor by our power, but it's God's spirit that draws people to Him.

Don't live a self-righteous lie, thinking lost souls that don't matter to us don't matter to God. Every person matters to God, and we are responsible for sharing the gospel with them. Ask God to give you a tender conscience by giving you a heart of compassion for the lost. Always be aware that God can and will speak through you, including when, where, and how to share His love with others. Thank Him for the privilege of sharing His love with those who don't already know Him.

Are you that person? Nothing makes you happy, and your negativity rubs off on others. You are mad, grumpy, and complaining about everything, and the joy of others irritates you. Is your misery wanting company, trying to pull others into your agony? We don't always see ourselves the way we are, so ask God to show you what's inside and how to change any hard-hearted attitude you might have towards others. Lean on God's strength and guidance as you change for His glory. Get rid of any pride or unwillingness that stands in the way of God's love for someone. Knowing someone received salvation is the greatest miracle that God has to offer. That alone should be enough to make anyone celebrate and be happy.

There is something wrong with us when we hate the success of others or covet what they have. Don't be a person whose heart remains unteachable. In spite of all that Jonah went through, he never appeared to have a heart change. We only see a six-day snapshot of Jonah's life; hopefully, he didn't live the rest of his life opposing God. He was too stubborn and defiant for his own good. No, thanks to living in the slimy, stinky belly of a fish or going through some other extreme measure before God gets our attention.

We have to remember that this earth is not our home. The only thing that matters in this life is how we live for God. We have a higher purpose: to bring as many people to know God as we can. Step back and regain your fight for Christ. Shine your light so that others will want to know the God you know. We are told in the Word that if God is lifted up, He will draw all men unto Himself.

Telling others about the love of Jesus is what God wants from all of His children. We are called to be His hands and feet and spread the love of God to unbelievers. Showing love to others is not cramming what we believe down someone's throat. We are not called to choose the results of any decisions others make. It's up to them to seek God or not. My job is to lovingly show them the way. Pray when witnessing to others that you don't become a stumbling block because you haven't prepared your heart to say what God wants you to say.

When God puts a call on your life, He tailors it to fit only you. His purpose and plan for our lives only work for our good if we obey, and only then will we truly be happy. Pay attention to God's voice in your heart as He guides you with His love and peace to do whatever He wants you to do. David could not go to fight Goliath in Saul's armor; he could only defeat the giant Philistine by going in the name of the Lord. We were not created to be someone else, so be the best you that God has created you to be.

God is not calling us to live a perfect life, but our actions speak louder than we know. Do others see you seeking after the things of God, willing to change for His glory? Or are you living in the fast lane of life while heading for unseen disasters? Out of the abundance of our hearts is what we speak. Have you given your mouth over for correction, or does it not matter to you what you say? Are you speaking about the good things of God so that others can see His glory in you? We can't expect God to honor us by saying whatever we want or living however we want.

When God calls us for His purposes, He can call someone else if we're not willing to obey, which was not the case for Jonah. We see him groveling and whining for God's sympathy, giving his reasons why he shouldn't have to obey. It didn't work for Jonah, so don't count on it working for you. He loves us too much to let us get away with our pathetic attitude or excuses. When we are told to do something for God, it is for our good or for the good of others.

To maintain a healthy relationship that pleases God, read His word daily, talk to Him, learn to hear His voice, and do what He tells you to do. God did not make us robots; we can choose to accept Him or not, and we can choose to obey Him or not. We become skilled craftsmen, ignoring, pretending not to hear, or trying to justify our bad behavior by convincing ourselves that we don't have to do what God wants us to do.

PRAYING FOR OTHERS

When praying for others, ask God to help them hit rock bottom so that they have nowhere else to turn but to God. Ask God to give someone a soft heart so that they can hear a message of hope and salvation. Pray that the person in need of salvation will have ears to hear, helping them to receive and understand the message that God has for them. Also, believe that if someone is not willing to listen to you, pray that God will send someone they will listen to who can tell them of His love. If there is no one, then ask God to send angels their way, whatever it takes. Our job is to pray for others and let them know about God's love, not try to control the outcome.

ASKING FOR FORGIVENESS

God will send others into your life, giving you the opportunity to know Him. He loves you so much that He sent Jesus to pay for your sins. God will never take your free will from you. He allows us to choose His goodness or reject it. AFTER THIS LIFE IS OVER, FOREVER, you will live either in the land of God's glory or in eternal damnation of torment and darkness. Jesus came and died so that you could spend eternity in heaven with Him.

Anyone **can come to Father God through Jesus, His son.** Hopefully, if you don't know Jesus, you are inspired to have a personal relationship with Him. All you have to do is ask for His forgiveness for your sins. Then ask Him to come into your life and help you change for His glory. You don't have to pray an elaborate prayer. A simple prayer from the heart is all it takes to be accepted by the one who loves you. We all fall short of His glory, and Jesus was sent to die for anyone who chooses to believe.

PRAYER OF SALVATION

Dear Jesus, come into my life and forgive me of my sins. Come into my heart and show me that you are real, and cleanse me from all unrighteousness. Thank you for dying on the cross for me and saving me from my sins. Amen

Your next step is to find a Bible-believing church to go to, one where you can go with a Bible and learn about God, Jesus, and the Holy Spirit. Pray and ask God to show you where He wants you to go.

PRAYER

Heavenly Father,

Thank you for pouring out your love and rescuing me from everlasting destruction. Thank you to all who have ever prayed for me or told me about you. Thank you for tugging at my heart and not giving up on me, an unworthy sinner. Help me not to ever take you for granted. The same love you poured out on me is the same love you want to share with others. People who don't know you and aren't concerned about what's right or wrong need you. I want to demonstrate your peace that passes all understanding so that your love will shine brightly in me, causing others to want to seek you. I need your help. I don't ever want to think more highly of myself than I should, or that I have the right to decide who deserves your love and who doesn't. If you call me to be a witness for someone in a place where I don't want to be, remind me that you have me there for your purposes and not mine. Show me how to have more compassion for the lost. I may be the only one who can share your love in a way that someone will receive it. God, do whatever needs to be done in me and cause my hard heart to be softened so that I will have compassion toward others. I repent of how little compassion I sometimes feel for others who don't live up to my standards. Renew a right spirit within me. My sympathy level sometimes runs on empty, causing judgment to flow from my lips. Let me see others the way you see them: as lost souls in need of a redeemer to rescue them from sin. Please help me to stay away from a self-righteous attitude, as my own righteousness is as filthy rags to you. I want to stay humble so that others will want to know about you. Guide me to your word every day so that I have your well of wisdom to draw from. Help me keep my smug opinions to myself. Draw me close to you as I strive to live a life that pleases you and not myself. Lead and guide me in the direction I should go. I want to carry your love to the lost souls that don't know you. Let others see you and not me if I'm having a bad day or attitude. I want to keep on your straight and narrow path and stay away from the many distractions this world has to offer. I can only have your unspeakable joy and love if I keep my eyes fixed on you. I want you to be the sunshine of my life. The prize I am seeking is heaven; nothing this world offers compares to you. When my compassion and patience levels are empty, help me remember your love for me and that I am to carry that love to others. I never want to see the day you stop talking to me because I have given up on you. You chased Jonah down until he obeyed, and I give you permission to chase me down and hound me until I obey. Teach me to pray blessings upon those that I feel are unworthy of your love. I need to be reminded that I am just as unworthy of your love as anyone else. Thank you in Jesus' name. Amen

SCRIPTURE REFERENCE: (KJV)

"And he answered and said, Must I not take heed to speak that which the LORD hath put in my mouth?" Numbers 23:12

"Know therefore this day, and consider it in thine heart, that the LORD he is God in heaven above, and upon the earth beneath: there is none else." Deuteronomy 4:39

"Be strong and of a good courage, fear not, nor be afraid of them: for the LORD thy God, he it is that doth go with thee; he will not fail thee, nor forsake thee." Deuteronomy 31:6

"And Samuel said, Hath the LORD as great delight in burnt offerings and sacrifices, as in obeying the voice of the LORD? Behold, to obey is better than sacrifice, and to hearken than the fat of rams." 1 Samuel 15:22

"And David girded his sword upon his armour, and he assayed to go; for he had not proved it. And David said unto Saul, I cannot go with these; for I have not proved them. And David put them off him." "Then said David to the Philistine, Thou comest to me with a sword, and with a spear, and with a shield: but I come to thee in the name of the LORD of hosts, the God of the armies of Israel, whom thou hast defied." "And all this assembly shall know that the LORD saveth not with sward and spear: for the battle is the LORD'S, and he will give you into our hands." 1 Samuel 17:39; 45; 47

"And after the earthquake a fire; but the LORD was not in the fire: and after the fire a still small voice." 1 Kings 19:12

"And call upon me in the day of trouble: I will deliver thee, and thou shalt glorify me." Psalms 50:15

"Enter into his gates with thanksgiving, and into his courts with praise: be thankful unto him, and bless his name." Psalms 100:4

"Search me, O God, and know my heart: try me, and know my thoughts:" "And see if there be any wicked way in me, and lead me in the way everlasting." Psalms 139:23-24

"Trust in the LORD with all thine heart; and lean not unto thine own understanding." "In all thy ways acknowledge him, and he shall direct thy paths." "My son, despise not the chastening of the LORD; neither be weary of his correction:" "For whom the LORD loveth he correcteth; even as a father the son in whom he delighteth." Proverbs 3:5-6; 11-12

"The fear of the LORD is the beginning of wisdom: and the knowledge of the holy is understanding." Proverbs 9:10

"Proverty and shame shall be to him that refuseth instruction: but he that regardeth reproof shall be honoured." Proverbs 13:18

"There is a way which seemth right unto a man, but the end thereof are the ways of death." Proverbs 14:12

"The eyes of the LORD are in every place, beholding the evil and the good." "A man hath joy by the answer of his mouth: and a word spoken in due season, how good is it!" Proverbs 15:3; 23

"Pleasant words are as an honeycomb, sweet to the soul, and health to the bones." Proverbs 16:24

"A brother offended is harder to be won than a strong city: and their contentions are like the bars of a castle." "Death and life are in the power of the tongue: and they that love it shall eat the fruit thereof." Proverbs 18:19; 21

"Every way of a man is right in his own eyes: but the LORD pondereth the hearts." Proverbs 21:2

"Thus saith the LORD the King of Israel, and his redeemer the LORD of hosts; I am the first, and I am the last; and beside me there is no God." Isaiah 44:6

"The Lord God hath given me the tongue of the learned, that I should know how to speak a word in season to him that is weary: he wakeneth morning by morning, he wakeneth mine ear to hear as the learned." Isaiah 50:4

"Let the wicked forsake his way, and the unrighteous man his thoughts: and let him return unto the LORD, and he will have mercy upon him; and to our God, for he will abundantly pardon." "For my thoughts are not your thoughts, neither are your ways my ways, saith the LORD." Isaiah 55:7-8

"Before I formed thee in the belly I knew thee; and before thou camest forth out of the womb I sanctified thee, and I ordained thee a prophet unto the nations." Jeremiah 1:5

"When I say unto the wicked, Thou shalt surely die; and thou givest him not warning, nor speakest to the wicked from his wicked way, to save his life; the same wicked man shall die in his iniquity; but his blood will I require at thine hand." Ezekiel 3:18

"Then he answered and spake unto me, saying, This is the word of the LORD unto Zerubbabel, saying, Not by might, nor by power, but by my spirit, saith the LORD of hosts." Zechariah 4:6

"Ye are the salt of the earth: but if the salt have lost his savour, wherewith shall it be salted? it is thenceforth good for nothing, but to be cast out, and to be trodden under foot of men." "Ye are the light of the world. A city that is set on a hill cannot be hid." "Let you light so shine before men, that they may see your good works, and glorify your Father which is in heaven." Matthew 5:13; 14; 16

"But thou, when thou prayest, enter into thy closet, and when thou hast shut they door, pray to thy Father which is in secret; and thy Father which seeth in secret shall reward they openly." Matthew 6:6

"Enter ye in at the straight gate: for wide is the gate, and broad is the way, that leadeth to destruction, and many there be which go in thereat:" Matthew 7:13

"For it is not ye that speak, but the Spirit of your Father which speaketh in you." Matthew 10:20

"But I say unto you, That every idle word that men shall speak, they shall give account thereof in the day of judgment." Matthew 12:36

"For I will give you a mouth and wisdom, which all your adversaries shall not be able to gainsay nor resist." Luke 21:15

"For God so loved the world, that he gave his only begotten Son, that whosoever believeth in him should not perish, but have everlasting life." John 3:16

"The thief cometh not, but for to steal, and to kill, and to destroy: I am come that they might have life, and that they might have it more abundantly." John 10:10

"And I, if I be lifted up from the earth, will draw all men unto me." John 12:32

"Jesus saith unto him, I am the way, the truth, and the life: no man cometh unto the Father, but by me." John 14:6

"Abide in me. and I in you. As the branch cannot bear fruit of itself, except it abide in the vine; no more can ye, except ye abide in me." "I am the vine, ye are the branches: He that abideth in me, and I in him, the same bringeth forth much fruit: for without me ye can do nothing." John 15:4-5

"For all have sinned, and come short of the glory of God;" Romans 3:23

"By whom also we have access by faith into this grace wherein we stand, and rejoice in hope of the glory of God." Romans 5:2

"And we know that all things work together for good to them that love God, to them who are called according to his purpose." Romans 8:28

"Well; because of unbelief they were broken off, and thou standest by faith. Be not highminded, but fear:" "For the gifts and calling of God are without repentance." Romans 11:20; 29

"Be of the same mind one toward another. Mind not high things, but condescend to men of low estate. Be not wise in your own conceits." "Dearly beloved, avenge not yourselves, but rather give place unto wrath: for it is written, Vengeance is mine; I will repay, saith the Lord." Romans 12:16; 19

"So then every one of us shall give account of himself to God." Romans 14:12

"So then neither is he that planted any thing, neither he that watereth; but God that giveth the increase." 1 Corinthians 3:7

"But take heed lest by any means this liberty of yours become a stumblingblock to them that are weak." 1 Corinthians 8:9

"For if a man think himself to be something, when he is nothing, he deceiveth himself." Galatians 6:3

"And grieve not the holy Spirit of God, whereby ye are sealed unto the day of redemption." Ephesians 4:30

"Be careful for nothing; but in every thing by prayer and supplication with thanksgiving let your requests be made known unto God." "And the peace of God, which passeth all understanding, shall keep your hearts and minds through Christ Jesus." Philippians 4:6-7

"I can do all things through Christ which strengtheneth me." Philippians 4:13

"Let your speech be alway with grace, seasoned with salt, that ye may know how ye ought to answer every man." Colossians 4:6

"In every thing give thanks: for this is the will of God in Christ Jesus concerning you." 1Thessalonians 5:18

"If a man therefor purge himself from these, he shall be a vessel unto honour, sanctified, and meet for the master's use, and prepared unto every good work" 2 Timothy 2:21

"All scripture is given by inspiration of God, and is profitable for doctrine, for reproof, for correction for instruction in righteousness:" 2 Timothy 3:16

"Preach the word; be instant in season, out of season; reprove, rebuke, exhort with all longsuffering and doctrine." "If a man therefore purge himself from these, he shall be a vessel unto honour, sanctified, and meet for the master's use, and prepared unto every good work." 2 Timothy 4:2; 21

Printed in the United States
by Baker & Taylor Publisher Services